Abstracts of Contested Estate Cases

Newfoundland: 1817-1949

Compiled by Lynne Butler, BA LLB

HOW TO FIND SOMEONE IN THIS COLLECTION:

1. First, use the alphabetical index in part 1 of this book to search for a name. Each name is followed by a number. In some cases there is more than one number.

2. The number following a name is a record number. It is NOT a page number.

3. Second, look up the record number(s) in part 2 of this book.

HOW THE RECORDS ARE SET UP:

1. The name of the case as it shows up in the court reports.

2. The date the case was reported. The date of the reported case is not the same as the date of death. In some cases, many years have passed from the date of death until a matter ended up in court. Early cases, in particular, did not always mention the date of death. We have included it in the collection if the case report included it.

3. The name of the deceased person as it is given in the case report. Full names of parties are not always given in the case reports. In some cases, parties are only referred to by surnames. First names and/or initials are included in this book when they are disclosed by the case reports. We do not guess or fill in the blanks, but simply show you what the court recorded.

4. The date of death, if it is stated in the case report. Not every case gives the date. In some cases, the full date is given and in others, only a year of death is given.

5. Names of any other people who are identified by name in the case report. You will also see each person's relationship to the deceased person, if that is given in the case report. These can be spouse, children, siblings, parents, friends, executors, witnesses or business partners.

6. A one or two sentence summary of the case.

7. Finding information for locating the full text of the case online.

WHAT TO DO WITH THE INFORMATION YOU FIND HERE:

The records included here may give you additional dates and names to add to your family tree.

After reading the contents of this book, you may choose to find and read the full text of the case that mentions your ancestor. By doing so, you may find additional information about your ancestor such as his or her occupation, town of residence, dates that other parties passed away, details about family who relocated, businesses, or family properties.

The finding information given in these records will guide you directly to the full cases. All of them can be found online at the Memorial University (MUN) Digital Archives.

Part 1:

Alphabetical Index of Names

Part 2:

Numbered Records

1   Name of case: In the Matter of John McGrath's Will

Date of case: August, 1821

Name of deceased: John McGrath

Date of death: Not given in the report

Other people named: Mr. Pendergast, executor; James Fox, executor.

Summary: Pendergast brought action for Fox to account for estate funds held in trust for Fox's children and to have funds invested in public investments.

Location: Decisions of the Supreme Court of NL 1817-1828, page 243

2   Name of case: John Williams vs. Thos. Williams et al

Date of case: February, 1818

Name of deceased: J. Monier

Date of death: Not given in the report

Other people named:Mary Monier, daughter; George Williams, son-in-law; John Williams, grandson; Thomas Williams, grandson.

Summary: Monier died leaving estate to Mary and her heirs. May and George died without wills. John tried to claim Mary's whole estate as her heir per British law.

Location: Decisions of the Supreme Court of NL 1817-1828, page 103

3   Name of case: George Heath et al vs. Robert Kean

Date of case: January, 1820

Name of deceased: William Kean, Sr

Date of death: Not given in the report

Other people mentioned: Benjamin Kean, son; Robert Kean, son; William Kean Jr., son; Martha Kean, granddaughter; George Heath, executor.

Summary: Kean died with a will dated 1772. Plantations in NL were divided among the 3 sons. Question over who owned land.

Location: Decisions of the Supreme Court of NL 1817-1828, page 193

4   Name of case: In Re Crawford & Co's Insolvency

Date of case: January, 1818

Name of deceased: John Crawford

Date of death: Not given in the report

Other people mentioned: Jean Crawford, widow and executor; James Crawford, son; Andrew Crawford, son; Joseph Tucker Crawford, son.

Summary: Crawford died with a will leaving income-producing property to wife and the rest to his 8 children. The property became insolvent. Wife claiming money from sons involved in the property.

Location: Decisions of the Supreme Court of NL 1817-1828, page 85

5   Name of case: Meagher & Morris vs. Flannery

Date of case: January, 1819

Name of deceased: Mr Barry

Date of death: Not given in the report

Other people mentioned: James Macbraire, executor; Mr. Flannery, tenant.

Summary: Barry died. Executor tried to evict over-holding tenant. Sued for unpaid rent.

Location: Decisions of the Supreme Court of NL 1817-1828, page 150

6 Name of case: Martha Rowe, administratrix vs. the heirs of Thomas Street

Date of case: March ,1820

Name of deceased: Thomas Street

Date of death: Not given in the report

Other people mentioned: James Rowe, business associate; Martha Rowe, widow of James.

Summary: Action to recover a fishing room and 5 years' rent.

Location: Decisions of the Supreme Court of NL 1817-1828, page 213

7 Name of case: William Legg vs. McCarthy & Banfield

Date of case: February, 1818

Name of deceased: Henry Webber

Date of death: Not given in the report

Other people mentioned: Francis Tucker, beneficiary; Dr Ferrers, tenant; Henry Tucker, son of Francis.

Summary: Webber died with a will dated 1769. Left property in Carbonear to Francis Tucker. She leased it to Dr. Ferrers. He overheld the term of the lease and she got a judgment for annual rent.

Location: Decisions of the Supreme Court of NL 1817-1828, page 112

8 Name of case: Chancey vs. Brooking, Administrator of the estate of John Murphy

Date of case: June, 1823

Name of deceased: John Murphy.

Date of death: Not given in the report

Summary: Action to recover rent for the occupation of a fishing room.

Location: Decisions of the Supreme Court of NL 1817-1828, page 314

9   Name of case: Dixon vs. Bennett

Date of case: August, 1848

Name of deceased: William Dixon

Date of death: 1839

Other people mentioned: Ms Dixon, daughter; Mr. Bennett, creditor of the deceased and administrator of the estate.

Summary: Dixon died in debt to Bennett. Bennett evicted widow and daughter from his premises. Daughter sought accounting of the estate and ownership of premises.

Location: Decisions of the Supreme Court of NL, 1846-1853, page 41

10   Name of case: Doe Dem Supple vs. Burton

Date of case: August, 1849

Name of deceased: Mr. Walsh

Date of death: Not given in the report

Other people mentioned: Mr. Supple, executor of the estate; Mr. Carter, lessor of the plaintiff.

Summary: A dispute over land owned by Walsh but leased by Carter for 20 years was awarded to Carter. Question as to who should pay costs.

Location: Decisions of the Supreme Court of NL, 1846-1853, page 100

11   Name of case: Widdicombe (Doe Dem) vs. Brazil

Date of case: July, 1851

Name of deceased: John Widdicombe

Date of death: Not given in the report

Other people mentioned: Mary Widdicombe, widow and administratrix.

Summary: Three lawsuits over time were brought by a lessor of Widdicombes against the same people over the same property. Issue of whether costs of one must be paid before third one could proceed.

12   Name of case: Re Estate of Michael Cullen

Date of case: September, 1852

Name of deceased: Michael Cullen

Date of death: Not given in the report

Other people mentioned: Margaret Cullen, daughter; Moses Cullen, son; Mr. Maguire, witness to will; John Cullen, son.

Summary: Deceased made a will shortly before death but will couldn't be found. Witnesses re-created it from memory. Court granted Administration CTA.

Location: Decisions of the Supreme Court of NL, 1846-1853, page 308

13   Name of case: Doe Dem Burton vs. Parker & Gleeson

Date of case: 1852

Name of deceased: Sarah Burton and Mr. Burton

Date of death: Sarah 1817; Mr Burton 1848

Other people mentioned: Philip Breenlan, witness to Sarah's will; John Norcomb, witness to Sarah's will; Joseph Gill, witness to Sarah's will; Lewis K. Ryan, witness to Sarah's codicil; Gabriel V. Mott, witness to Sarah's codicil.

Summary: Under Sarah's will, land was left to son, who died in 1848. Dispute with lessor of property. Question whether Sarah's will had been probated and reference to the court's official wills book of records.

Location: Decisions of the Supreme Court of NL, 1846-1853, page 310

14   Name of case: Gushue vs. Norman & Gushue (exrs.)

Date of case: 1852

Name of deceased: Mr. Gushue

Date of death: June 19, 1826

Other people mentioned: Mr. Gushue, son.

Summary: Will directed the trustees to care for his widow according to their discretion, with the son to inherit when he turned 21. Trustees invested poorly and lost money.

Location: Decisions of the Supreme Court of NL, 1846-1853, page 252

15   Name of case: McKinley (Doe Dem) vs. Elliott

Date of case: July, 1851

Name of deceased: Mr. Molton

Date of death: 1834

Other people mentioned: Mr. McKinley, lessor; Mr. Troke, son-in-law; Mr. Falle, purchaser of property.

Summary: Question whether a property transfer made by the administrator of the estate before getting letters of administration was valid.

Location: Decisions of the Supreme Court of NL, 1846-1853, page 180

16   Name of case: In Re Estate Martin Walsh, Deceased

Date of case: June, 1921

Name of deceased: Martin Walsh

Date of death: Not given in the report

Other people mentioned: Ellen Cole, sister; Bridget Cole, niece; Catherine Power, niece; Robert Cole, nephew.

Summary: Over time, all beneficiaries of an annuity passed away. Question whether the annuity is perpetual and therefore payable to the estate of the last beneficiary.

Location: Decisions of the Supreme Court of NL, 1921-1926, page 62

17   Name of case: In Re William Brazil's Estate

Date of case: January, 1925

Name of deceased: William Brazil, Alice Taylor, Thomas Brazil, William Brazil,

David Brazil, Patrick Brazil, and Catherine Donnelly

Date of death: William April,1897; Alice July 1899; Thomas November 1899; William October 1909; David September 1911; Patrick June 1915; Catherine April 1916

Other people mentioned: Alice Taylor, daughter; Catherine Donnelly, daughter; Fergus Donnelly, son-in-law; Margaret Brazil, daughter; Olive Christian, grand-child; Gladys O'Leary, grand-child; Thomas Brazil, son; William Brazil, son; David Brazil, son; Patrick Brazil, son.

Summary: Interpretation of an unclear clause in a will.

Location: Decisions of the Supreme Court of NL, 1921-1926, page 381

18   Name of case: Re Will of Daniel Monroe; David M. Baird et al vs. Pamela Alderdice et al

Date of case: December 5, 1921

Name of deceased: Norman H. Alderdice

Date of death: May 12, 1917

Other people mentioned: None

Summary: Where the war office has presumed a missing soldier to be dead, the court doesn't require a formal application to declare him to be dead.

Location: Decisions of the Supreme Court of NL, 1921-1926, page 70

19   Name of case: Kennedy, In Re Lawrence, Deceased

Date of case: March, 1923

Name of deceased: Lawrence Kennedy

Date of death: May, 1921

Other people mentioned: Annie Malone, daughter and administratrix; Margaret Malone, granddaughter.

Summary: Deceased gave a bank book to his daughter shortly before his death. Question whether he intended it to be a joint account with her.

Location: Decisions of the Supreme Court of NL, 1921-1926, page 251

20   Name of case: Higgins vs. Noseworthy, Administrator of Noseworthy

Date of case: June, 1924

Name of deceased: Ernest Noseworthy

Date of death: 1922

Other people mentioned: Ms. Higgins, sister.

Summary: The deceased owned a joint bank account. Question was whether he intended it to be paid to the other owner as surviving joint owner.

Location: Decisions of the Supreme Court of NL, 1921-1926, page 327

21   Name of case: In Re The Death Duties Act and In Re Will of Hugh Baird, Deceased

Date of case: June, 1923

Name of deceased: Hugh Baird

Date of death: February, 1922

Other people mentioned: None

Summary: On appeal of the Minister of Finance's valuation of the deceased's estate, question regarding whether the Minister could be held liable for costs.

Locaton: Decisions of the Supreme Court of NL, 1921-1926, page 292

22   Name of case: In Re The Death Duties Act and In Re Will of Hugh Baird, Deceased

Date of case: March, 1923

Name of deceased: Hugh Baird

Date of death: February, 1922

Other people mentioned: Madeline Baird, James Baird and Royal Trust Co, executors of the estate.

Summary: Question whether a large corporate dividend from James Baird Limited was part of the estate.

Location: Decisions of the Supreme Court of NL, 1921-1926, page 239

23   Name of case:In Re Estate of James A. Reid and In Re Death Duties Act

Date of case: October 21, 1921

Name of deceased: James A. Reid

Date of death: Not given in the report

Other people mentioned: None

Summary: Appeal from the valuation of the Minister of Finance.

Location: Decisions of the Supreme Court of NL, 1921-1926, page 65

24   Name of case: McKay, Appellant vs. US Fidelity Guarantee Co., Respondent

Date of case: October, 1926

Name of deceased: William A. McKay

Date of death: December 6, 1925

Other people mentioned: Mrs. McKay, mother.

Summary: Where a claim is made that the death of an insured person was the result of an accident, it must be shown that the death was in fact the result of an accident. Mere possibility is not enough.

Location: Decisions of the Supreme Court of NL, 1921-1926, page 579

25   Name of case: Robert G. Reid vs. Sir William Reid

Date of case: April 28, 1921

Name of deceased: Sir Robert Gillespie Reid

Date of death: Not given in the report

Other people mentioned: Robert G. Reid, son; Royal Trust Co., executor of the estate.

Summary: A creditor was entitled to ¼ share of the estate but the value had not been ascertained. Question whether unascertained share could be attachable as chose in action.

Location: Decisions of the Supreme Court of NL, 1921-1926, page 42

26   Name of case: Robert Reid, Appellant vs. William Reid, Respondent

Date of case: May 9, 1921

Name of deceased: Sir Robert Gillespie Reid

Date of death: Not given in the report

Other people mentioned: Royal Trust Co., executor of the estate.

Summary: Unsuccessful appeal of decision of April 28, 1921.

Location: Decisions of the Supreme Court of NL, 1921-1926, page 46

27   Name of case: Doe Dem Evans vs. Doyle, Executor

Date of case: January, 1860

Name of deceased: Mary Evans Doyle

Date of death: 1858

Other people mentioned: Joseph Butler, father; Robert Evans, first husband; Mr. Doyle, second husband; James Doyle, executor of the estate; John Evans, son.

Summary: Question of who was to own a plantation gifted to the deceased by her father and passed down to her children.

Location: Decisions of the Supreme Court of NL, 1854-1864, page 432

28   Name of case: Norman vs. Gushue

Date of case: January, 1854

Name of deceased: Mr. Gushue

Date of death: Not given in the report

Other people mentioned: John Gushue, son, defendant; Mr. Norman, executor of the estate.

Summary: There was a verdict against the executors for breach of trust and other matters. Only one executor paid. Question whether that executor could force the other one to contribute.

Location: Decisions of the Supreme Court of NL, 1854-1864, page 29

28   Name of case: In Re Estate of James Barr

Date of case: January, 1863

Name of deceased: James Barr

Date of death: 1860

Other people mentioned: William Henry Mare, administrator of the estate; Theodore Clift, commission merchant; Thomas McKen, creditor; J.W. Prowse, creditor; Estate of Alex Mills, creditor; J.C. Toussaint, creditor.

Summary: When an estate does not have enough assets to pay all debts, the administrator may ask the court for an order of distribution of the estate.

Location: Decisions of the Supreme Court of NL, 1854-1864, page 715

29   Name of case: Bearns vs. Noad et al

Date of case: January, 1854

Name of deceased: George Lilly

Date of death: Not given in the report

Other people mentioned: Mr. Noad, executor of the estate; Emma Gaden, assignor.

Summary: When a person gives his representative power of sale and the representative dies, the power does not transfer to his heirs or executors.

Location: Decisions of the Supreme Court of NL, 1854-1864, page 33

30   Name of case: In Re the Will of Patrick Doyle

Date of case: January, 1858

Name of deceased: Patrick Doyle

Date of death: Not given in the report

Other people mentioned: Rev. John Thomas Mullock, executor of the estate; Hon. John Kent, executor of the estate.

Summary: The idea of making a will does not have to originate with the testator as long as the testator understands and approves of the contents of the will.

Location: Decisions of the Supreme Court of NL, 1854-1864, page 183

31 Name of case: In Re the Will of William Callahan

Date of case: January, 1859

Name of deceased: William Callahan

Date of death: Not given in the report

Other people mentioned: Rev. Dr. John Dalton, preparer of the will; James Callahan, cousin; David Kenealy, witness; Martin Callahan, brother, administrator of the estate.

Summary: The will was lost. The only witness called to support its contents was the main beneficiary as well as the person who drew up the will and later mislaid it. The will was admitted to probate.

Location: Decisions of the Supreme Court of NL, 1854-1864, page 276

32 Name of case: In Re the Will of John Hennebury

Date of case: January, 1859

Name of deceased: John Hennebury

Date of death: Not given in the report

Other people mentioned: None

Summary: If there is no evidence at all of the execution of a lost will, it cannot be admitted to probate.

Location: Decisions of the Supreme Court of NL, 1854-1864, page 288

33 Name of case: In Re Will of Elizabeth Haye

Date of case: January, 1858

Name of deceased: Elizabeth Haye

Date of death: 1856

Other people mentioned: George Anderson, witness; Harcourt Mooney, Esq., preparer of the will; Elizabeth Anderson, god-daughter, beneficiary; Mary Ann Winter, beneficiary.

Summary: When a will is lost, it is not necessary to have two witnesses as to its contents. One is sufficient if corroborated on material points.

Location: Decisions of the Supreme Court of NL, 1854-1864, page 227

34   Name of case: In Re Will of John Brocklebank

Date of case: January, 1856

Name of deceased: John Brocklebank

Date of death: December 14, 1852

Other people mentioned: Annie Brocklebank, widow; Matthew William Wall-bank, lawyer, preparer of will; David Steele, Esq., witness; Kenneth McLea, Esq., executor; Patrick Tasker, executor; John Toomey, beneficiary; Catherine Mahony, beneficiary; Ellen Barron, beneficiary; Mary Gordon, sister, beneficiary; William Leight Anthony, Esq., beneficiary; Charles Simms, Esq., witness; Nathaniel Thomas, witness; Anastasia Lane, nurse, witness; Dr. Kielly, witness; John Stuart, Esq., witness; Thomas Glen, Esq., witness; Robert Alsop, Esq., witness; Richard O'Dwyer, Esq., witness; Robert Gray, Esq., cousin of Annie, witness; Henry Simms, Esq., uncle of Annie, witness; Henry Holt, witness; Francis Hutchinson, Esq, witness; A.M. Adams, Esq., witness; William Marshall, Esq., witness; Alexander McCrackan, witness; Archibald Blacklock, witness; James Bendall, witness; Thomas Jackson, witness; William Primrose, witness; Edward George Janes, witness.

Summary: A party who tries to set aside a will on the grounds of insanity must do so by clear and satisfactory proof. The onus of proof is on the person challenging the will.

Location: Decisions of the Supreme Court of NL, 1854-1864, page 88

35   Name of case: In Re Will of Mary Doyle

Date of case: January, 1859

Name of deceased: Mary Doyle

Date of death: Not given in the report

Other people mentioned: None

Summary: When a married woman makes a will during the lifetime of her husband, it must be republished after his death before it can be admitted to probate.

Location: Decisions of the Supreme Court of NL, 1854-1864, page 403

36 Name of case: Doe Dem Prendergast vs. Beer, Administrator

Date of case: January, 1863

Name of deceased: Mr. Prendergast

Date of death: Not given in the report

Other people mentioned: None

Summary: When administration of an estate is granted by the court, the authority of the administrator goes back to the date of death.

Location:Decisions of the Supreme Court of NL, 1854-1864, page 751

37 Name of case: In Re Parker's Estate

Date of case: March, 1864

Name of deceased: Thomas Parker

Date of death: June 19, 1851

Other people mentioned: Charles Simms, executor.

Summary: An accounting by an executor may not conclude or embarrass the rights of beneficiaries.

Location: Decisions of the Supreme Court of NL, 1864-1874, page 17

38 Name of case: In re Estate of Thomas Parker

Date of case: July, 1864

Name of deceased: Thomas Parker

Date of death: June 19, 1851

Other people mentioned: Charles Simms, executor.

Summary: A new executor can be appointed where the named executor was unable to manage the estate due to health.

Location: Decisions of the Supreme Court of NL, 1864-1874, page 80

39   Name of case: Johanna Parker vs. Charles Simms

Date of case: May, 1864

Name of deceased: Thomas Parker

Date of death: June 19, 1851

Other people mentioned: Charles Simms, executor.

Summary: Irregularities in the executor's accounting necessitated court proceedings. Executor had to pay petitioner's costs.

Location: Decisions of the Supreme Court of NL, 1864-1874, page 37

40   Name of case: In Re Thomas Parker's Estate

Date of case: May, 1864

Name of deceased: Thomas Parker

Date of death: June 19, 1851

Other people mentioned: Charles Simms, executor;

Summary: Unsatisfactory accounting by executor and refusal to produce books of account. Court would not disallow executor's pension or disallow sale of property.

Location: Decisions of the Supreme Court of NL, 1864-1874, page 23

41   Name of case: Reddin, Administrator vs. Stafford, Executor

Date of case: July, 1871

Name of deceased: Laurence O'Brien

Date of death: 1870

Other people mentioned: Margaret Annie (Hawe) Reddin, niece; Mary Josephine (Hawe) Quill, sister-in-law; George Hayward, witness.

Summary: Question about whether debentures held by a family member then sold had been held in trust for nieces.

Location: Decisions of the Supreme Court of NL, 1864-1874, page 389

42 Name of case: In re Insolvency of K. McLea & Sons

Date of case: July, 1868

Name of deceased: Kenneth McLea

Date of death: 1862

Other people mentioned: Henry K. Dickinson, trustee; Elizabeth Jane Walbank, daughter, beneficiary; Jeanie Catherine Prowse, daughter, beneficiary;Catherine Harriett MacRae, daughter, beneficiary; Robert Alsop, creditor; John Brine McLea, son, executor; Matthew William Wallbank, executor; Thomas R. Smith, executor; James S. McLea, son; Robert P. McLea, son; Elizabeth Brine, mother-in-law, beneficiary; Angus McInnes, witness; Thomas Winsborrow, witness; Robert Prowse, son-in-law.

Summary: Deceased left funds in a partnership with earnings paid to beneficiaries. Later the company went under. Question of whether the funds belonged to the estate.

Location: Decisions of the Supreme Court of NL, 1864-1874, page 228

43 Name of case: Whibby, a Minor vs. Wallbank, Administrator of Mary Whibby and Jas. Whibby

Date of case: July, 1869

Name of deceased: Mary (Malone) Whibby

Date of deceased: Not given in the report

Other people mentioned: Michael Anthony Whibby, deceased son; James Whibby, widower.

Summary: Wife who was separated from husband died intestate. Question whether her savings went to her son or her husband.

44 Name of case: Mandeville and Smith Mills, Executors of Margaret Whelan vs. Pinsent, Executor of Walter Whelan

Date of case: March, 1864

Name of deceased: Walter Whelan

Date of death: Not given in the report

Other people mentioned: Mr. Pinsent, executor; Margaret Whelan, wife and beneficiary.

Summary: Interpretation of an unclear clause in a will.

Location: Decisions of the Supreme Court of NL, 1864-1874, page 19

45 Name of case: Power et al vs. Menchinton, Administratrix

Date of case: July, 1869

Name of deceased: William Menchinton

Date of death: June 10, 1866

Other people mentioned: Grace Menchinton, widow, administratrix; Amelia Anne Menchinton, daughter; Mary Winser, daughter; James Winser, husband of Mary; Louisa Winser, daughter; Thomas Winser, husband of Louisa; Jane Gibbons, deceased daughter; William J.M. Gibbons, grandson, son of Jane; John Menchinton, deceased son.

Summary: Interpretation of an unclear clause in a will.

Location: Decisions of the Supreme Court of NL, 1864-1874, page 262

46 Name of case: Brown et al, Executors of Stephen Roberts vs. Roberts

Date of case: August, 1864

Name of deceased: Stephen Roberts

Date of death: Not given in the report

Other people mentioned: Stephen Alexander Roberts, son; Henry Percy Roberts, nephew; Jane Roberts, widow.

Summary: Interpretation of an unclear clause in a will.

Location: Decisions of the Supreme Court of NL, 1864-1874, page 83

47   Name of case: Wallbank, Administrator vs. Casey, Executor of Cuddihy

Date of case: July, 1870

Name of deceased: John Cuddihy

Date of death: 1841

Other people mentioned: Matthew Cuddihy, nephew, beneficiary; Edward Cuddihy, brother; Richard Cuddihy, nephew, beneficiary; John Cuddihy, nephew, beneficiary; Michael Cuddihy, son of Richard.

Summary: Interpretation of an unclear clause in a will.

Location: Decisions of the Supreme Court of NL, 1864-1874, page 363

48   Name of case: In re Will Patrick Tarrahan

Date of case: January, 1867

Name of deceased: Patrick Tarrahan

Date of death: August 7, 1866

Other people mentioned: Julia Tarrahan, widow; John Tarrahan, son; Patrick McGrath, nephew; Catherine Tarrahan, daughter.

Summary: Unusual attestation of the will, including testator using initials rather than name. Will was valid but clauses added later were not.

Location: Decisions of the Supreme Court of NL, 1864-1874, page 186

49   Name of case: In re Will of William Menchinton

Date of case: January, 1866

Name of deceased: William Menchinton

Date of death: June 10, 1866

Other people mentioned: Frederick R. Page, executor; J.G. Jeans, executor; John Power, son-in-law; Robert John Parson, Esq., witness; Amelia Power, daughter.

Summary: Will was read to blind testator with one witness in the room. Will held not to be valid.

Location: Decisions of the Supreme Court of NL, 1864-1874, page 159

50   Name of case: In the Goods of Ed. Doherty

Date of case: August, 1883

Name of deceased: Edward Doherty

Date of death: Not given in the report

Other people mentioned: Michael Doherty, brother; John Doherty, deceased brother.

Summary: When two brothers die in the same calamity, there is no presumption that one survived the other.

Location: Decisions of the Supreme Court of NL, 1874-1884, page 515

51   Name of case: Re Hennebury's Will

Date of case: February, 1880

Name of deceased: Mr. Hennebury

Date of death: Not given in the report

Other people mentioned: None

Summary: When proponents of a will under which they had taken legacies later called for proof in solemn form, the court refused their costs.

Location: Decisions of the Supreme Court of NL, 1874-1884, page 201

52   Name of case: In re Gibb's Estate

Date of case: December 1879

Name of deceased: Not given in the report

Date of death: Not given in the report

Other people mentioned: None

Summary: The Judges of the Supreme Court have power to prescribe the manner in which the Chief Clerk and Registrar runs his office.

Location: Decisions of the Supreme Court of NL, 1874-1884, page 196

53   Name of case: Hughes vs. Winser

Date of case: December, 1882

Name of deceased: Dr. Moran and Miss Eliza Moran

Date of death: Not given in the report

Other people mentioned: Rev. A.C. Winser, executor of Eliza; Mr. Hughes, brother-in-law of Eliza.

Summary: There must be delivery of, parting with, and then control over an item during the lifetime of the donor in order for it to be a deathbed gift.

Location: Decisions of the Supreme Court of NL, 1874-1884, page 461

54   Name of case: Carter, Administrator vs. Kelly

Date of case: January, 1882

Name of deceased: Mr. Mellor

Date of death: Not given in report

Other people mentioned: None

Summary: In order to be a deathbed gift, there must be transfer of possession of the item in contemplation of death.

Location: Decisions of the Supreme Court of NL, 1874-1884, page 370

55   Name of case: Greene vs. Greene

Date of case: March, 1881

Name of deceased: Rachel Greene

Date of death: 1877

Other people mentioned: John Greene, son; Daniel Greene, son.

Summary: Question whether son had given up a lease left to him by his mother.

Location: Decisions of the Supreme Court of NL, 1874-1884, page 287

56   Name of case: Newman et al vs. Simms, Administratrix, et al

Date of case: May, 1882

Name of deceased: Not given in the report

Date of death: Not given in the report

Other people mentioned: Fanny Simms, administratrix.

Summary: There can be no set-off of debts against a legacy unless they both refer to the same right.

Location: Decisions of the Supreme Court of NL, 1874-1884, page 422

57   Name of case: In re Bongard's Will

Date of case: January, 1881

Name of deceased; Mr. Bongard

Date of death: Not given in report

Summary: Will from Quebec. To prove it in NL, there should be a certificate from a Quebec judge that the will was valid where it was made.

Location: Decisions of the Supreme Court of NL, 1874-1884, page 255

58   Name of case: Percy vs. Norman, Administratrix

Date of case: December, 1881

Name of deceased: John Norman

Date of death: 1869

Other people mentioned: Robert J.C. Leamon, executor; Isaac Bartlett.

Summary: Where an executor withdraws funds as an agent of a legatee, the co-executor is safe from a lawsuit by the legatee.

Location: Decisions of the Supreme Court of NL, 1874-1884, page 360

59 Name of case: Dearin vs. Kough, Executor

Date of case: April, 1878

Name of deceased: James Furlong

Date of death: 1856

Other people mentioned: Elizabeth Furlong, daughter deceased in 1868; Mr. Kough, executor; Mr. Kavanagh, executor.

Summary: Question regarding whether a child was entitled to receive the share of his deceased parent, when the parent was a beneficiary.

Locaiton: Decisions of the Supreme Court of NL, 1874-1884, page 154

60 Name of case: Trustees of McLea vs. Executors of McLea

Date of case: March, 1875

Name of deceased: Kenneth McLea

Date of death: 1862

Other people mentioned: John B. McLea, son; James S. McLea, son; Robert P. McLea, son; Elizabeth McLea, daughter; Jeanie McLea, daughter; Catherine Mc-Lea, daughter.

Summary: The assignees of a bankrupt partnership were not entitled to the legacies bequeathed to them so long as the partnership was in debt to the estate.

Location: Decisions of the Supreme Court of NL, 1874-1884, page 37

61   Name of case In Re Will of Mary Anne Pike

Date of case: December, 1882

Name of deceased: Mary Anne Pike

Date of death: March, 1882

Other people mentioned: Stephen B. Pike; Lavinia Thompson; Robert Pike; Mrs. Erickson, daughter; Edward T. Pike, husband; Edward S. Pike, witness, executor; T. Bemister, executor; Mary Pike, witness, mother of Stephen.

Summary: A lost will may be proved by secondary evidence. One witness is sufficient in certain circumstances.

Location: Decisions of the Supreme Court of NL, 1874-1884, page 445

62   Name of case: Shortis vs. Kent, Executor

Date of case: March, 1877

Name of deceased: John Power

Date of death: April, 1872

Other people mentioned: Mrs. Shortis, sister, beneficiary; Mr. Kent, executor.

Summary: Whether beneficiary was entitled to shares that were declared as a bonus on original shares bequeathed to her for life.

Location: Decisions of the Supreme Court of NL, 1874-1884, page 138

63   Name of case: In re Will of Elvina Murray

Date of case: August, 1880

Name of deceased: Elvina Murray

Date of death: Not given in the report

Other people mentioned: Peter Payne, executor; Elizabeth (Carter) Payne, niece, executor, wife of Peter; Henry Radford, deceased father; Elizabeth Radford, mother; Lydia Murray, sister; William Murray, deceased husband; James Murray, brother-in-law, husband of Lydia; Elizabeth (Knox) Bone, niece of James; Robert Bone, husband of Elizabeth Bone; Susan Carter, niece; Charles Radford, brother; Sarah Radford, witness.

Summary: An alleged will document will not be probated where it is unsupported by sufficient evidence, especially when it is to claim title to property after an adverse possession with no claim for possession for over 30 years.

Location: Decisions of the Supreme Court of NL, 1874-1884, page 228

64 Name of case: In re Will of Richard Allen

Date of case: March, 1880

Name of deceased: Richard Allen

Date of death: October, 1879

Other people mentioned: Richard Clark; Rev. Theophilus Netten, executor; Henry G. Chafe, beneficiary, executor; David Chafe, witness; Mr. Rhodes, nephew, witness.

Summary: A person may have testamentary capacity despite having periods where his mind is inactive.

Location: Decisions of the Supreme Court of NL, 1874-1884, page 206

65 Name of case: Emerson (Executor) vs. Shortis

Date of case: May, 1881

Name of deceased: James Cahill

Date of death: August, 1878

Other people mentioned: Lewis W. Emerson, Esq., executor; Margaret Hartery, niece, beneficiary; Henry F. Shortis, nephew.

Summary: Funds obtained from an elderly person through undue influence had to be returned to the estate.

Location: Decisions of the Supreme Court of NL, 1874-1884, page 289

66 Name of case: Jackman, Administratrix vs. Walsh

Date of case: January, 1882

Name of deceased: John Mahoney

Date of death: Not given in the report

Other people mentioned: Martin Mahoney (aka Martin Meany, deceased father; Mrs. Jackman, administratrix of John; Nicholas Walsh, son-in-law of Martin; Johanna (Mahoney) Walsh, daughter of Martin, wife of Nicholas; Father Murphy, parish priest; Mr. Hayden, witness; Mr. Dutton, witness; Mr. Eagan, witness; Mr. Finn, witness; Denis Murphy, witness; Mortimer Murphy, witness; Thomas Kane, witness; Florence Murphy, witness; John Shaughnessy, witness.

Summary: None

Location: Decisions of the Supreme Court of NL, 1874-1884, page 367

67   Name of case: Morris vs. Murphy

Date of case: May, 1888

Name of deceased: Mrs. Murphy

Date of death: May 25, 1887

Other people mentioned: William Henry Murphy, son; Patrick Murphy, son; Michael Murphy, son; James Murphy, grandson, son of Michael; Peter Murphy, step-son; James Murphy, step-son; Margaret Murphy Tobin, daughter; William Tobin, husband of Margaret; John Murphy, son; Catherine Murphy Ryan, daughter; John Ryan, husband of Catherine; Anastatia Murphy Aylward, daughter; James Aylward, husband of Anastatia.

Summary: Mother left her home to her son. Question whether money found in the home was to be his as well.

Location: Decisions of the Supreme Court of NL, 1884-1896, Page 295

68   Name of case: In re Amelia Cairns, Browning vs. Winter, and In re Wm. J. Cairns, Cairns vs. Browning

Date of case: June 28, 1906 and October 8, 1906

Name of deceased: Amelia Cairns

Date of death: September 26, 1896

Other people mentioned: William J. Cairns, son; Robert C. Ayre and Walter S. Monroe, temporary administrators of Amelia's estate; Sir James Winter, court-appointed administrator of Amelia's estate; Donald M. Browning, court-appointed administrator of William's estate.

Summary: The estate of a mother could be distributed as if her son had died because he had not been heard from in 7 years.

Location: Decisions of the Supreme Court of NL, 1904-1911, page 187 and 189

69 Name of case: Leahy vs. O'Keefe, Administrator of Leahy

Date of case: May 1891

Name of deceased: Michael Leahy

Date of death: September, 1888

Other people mentioned: Anne O'Keefe, sister, administrator of the estate, wife of Robert O'Keefe; Mary Leahy, plaintiff, widow of Martin Leahy; Robert O'Keefe, brother-in-law, witness.

Summary: Question whether a bank receipt given to deceased's sister was a gift of the account to her.

Location: Decisions of the Supreme Court of NL, 1884-1896, page 527

70 Name of case: In re Joseph Drover

Date of case: April, 1885

Name of deceased: Joseph Drover

Date of death: March 10, 1883

Other people mentioned: Thomas Drover, brother, administrator of estate; Elizabeth Drover, widow; Susannah Drover Young, sister; John Young, brother-in-law; Mary Drover Lundrigan, sister; George Lundrigan, brother-in-law, husband of Mary; Mary Ann Drover Young, niece; Albert Young, husband of Mary Ann; Emma Drover Young, niece; Archibald Young, husband of Emma; Joseph Drover Young, grand-nephew (son of Emma).

Summary: Whether money held by the deceased in various accounts with other people were gifts to those account holders or part of the estate.

Location: Decisions of the Supreme Court of NL, 1884-1896, page 45

71 Name of case: Collins vs. Collins, Executor

Date of case: May, 1891

Name of deceased: John Collins

Date of death: 1854

Other people mentioned: James R. Collins, son, executor; James J. Callanan, purchase of property; Thomas D. Collins, son; Matilda Thomey, daughter.

Summary: Demand for accounting by executor, who was accused of planting bidders at auction of estate property.

Location: Decisions of the Supreme Court of NL, 1884-1896, page 549

72 Name of case: In re James Fitzgerald

Date of case: November, 1892

Name of deceased: James Fitzgerald

Date of death: January 10, 1891

Other people mentioned: William B. Fitzgerald, son, executor; Michael T. Fitzgerald, son; Ambrose T. Fitzgerald, son; J.T. Croucher, executor; Catherine Fitzgerald, wife of William; Bridget Gertrude Fitzgerald, daughter of William.

Summary: Question whether money was a gift to daughter-in-law and her children based on a verbal promise.

Location: Decisions of the Supreme Court of NL, 1884-1896, page 714

73 Name of case: Moore vs. Power

Date of case: October, 1890

Name of deceased: Bridget Tobin

Date of death: November, 1888

Other people mentioned: James Power, brother-in-law

Summary: Money was given to a servant. Later the servant returned the bankbook. Question whether this re-vested the money in the donor.

Location: Decisions of the Supreme Court of NL, 1884-1896, page 466

74   Name of case: In re Estate John Boone

Date of case: April, 1887

Name of deceased: John H. Boone

Date of death: November, 1884

Other people mentioned: James Baird, Esq., creditor;

Summary: Question whether a mortgage document signed before death was security for a debt.

Location: Decisions of the Supreme Court of NL, 1884-1896, page 196

75   Name of case: Browning v. Browning

Date of case: February, 1887

Name of deceased: James Browning

Date of death: Not given in the report

Other people mentioned: John Browning, brother; William Browning, brother.

Summary: Co-partner of business died. Administratrix wanted accounting that partners would not provide.

Location: Decisions of the Supreme Court of NL, 1884-1896, page 161

76   Name of case: In In re estate Neil MacDougall, Deceased

Date of case: March, 1884

Name of deceased: Neil MacDougall, Sr. and Neil MacDougall, Jr.

Date of death: Senior June 1875, Junior October, 1876

Other people mentioned: Laura Jane Nisbet, widow of the younger Neil Mac-Dougall; John MacDougall, son; Dougall MacDougall, son; Donald MacDougall, son; Henrietta MacDougall, daughter; Thomas MacDougall, son; Florence Mac-Dougall, daughter; Alexander Nisbet, 2nd husband of Laura Jane.

Summary: When a legatee dies before property vests in him, the other beneficiaries of the trust take the whole trust.

Location: Decisions of the Supreme Court of NL, 1884-1896, page 7

77   Name of case: In re the Will of John H. Warren

Date of case: April, 1886

Name of deceased: John H. Warren

Date of death: April, 1885

Other people mentioned: Adolph George Warren, son; Anne Warren, sister; Jane Elizabeth Warren, daughter; James S. Winter, executor for son Adolph's estate.

Summary: Question regarding interpretation of a clause of a will.

Location: Decisions of the Supreme Court of NL, 1884-1896, page 112

78   Name of case: In re Jacob Chafe

Date of case: February, 1887

Name of deceased: Jacob Chafe

Date of death: May 1878

Other people mentioned: David Chafe, brother-in-law, administrator of estate; Harriet Chafe, widow; Elizabeth Chafe, daughter; Ambrose Chafe, husband of Elizabeth; Henry George Chafe, son; Amelia Chafe, daughter; Thomas William Chafe, husband of Amelia.

Summary: Beneficiaries under an invalid will agreed to follow the will. Contested by those who would inherit on intestacy.

Location: Decisions of the Supreme Court of NL, 1884-1896, page 182

79   Name of case: In re Estate Charles Fox Bennett

Date of case: December, 1884

Name of deceased: Charles Fox Bennett

Date of death: Not given in the report

Other people mentioned: Thomas R. Smith, executor; Thomas Hutchings, beneficiary; Josephine Brettingham, sister-in-law; Sophia Stonehouse, sister-in-law; Rev. Arthur Stonehouse, brother-in-law.

Summary: Testator left an annuity but the annuitant died within the first year, thus receiving no payment from the annuity.

Location: Decisions of the Supreme Court of NL, 1884-1896, page 36

80 Name of case: In re Catherine Walsh

Date of case: April, 1893

Name of deceased: Catherine Walsh

Date of death: March 1892

Other people mentioned: John Walsh, son; Andrew Walsh, son; Francis Jackman, son-in-law; John Healy, witness.

Summary: The court held a will to be valid even though it was signed at the top and not the usual place near the bottom.

Location: Decisions of the Supreme Court of NL, 1884-1896, page 738

81 Name of case: In re Thomas Dunn

Date of case: July, 1885

Name of deceased: Thomas Dunn

Date of death: Not given in the report

Other people mentioned: Mr. Byrne, witness; Mr. Carew, witness.

Summary: A will was found to be invalid because only one witness signed in the presence of the testator and the other signed later.

Location: Decisions of the Supreme Court of NL, 1884-1896, page 82

82 Name of case: Trustees Finlay vs. Finlay

Date of case: February, 1888

Name of deceased: Jabez N. Finlay

Date of death: January, 1883

Other people mentioned: Elizabeth Sarah Finley, widow; Frederick William Finlay, son.

Summary: Bequest to a beneficiary who had been found to be bankrupt was given to his bankruptcy trustee.

Location: Decisions of the Supreme Court of NL, 1884-1896, page 262

83 Name of case: Winter vs. Budden

Date of case: April, 1884

Name of deceased: George Winter

Date of death: Not given in the report

Other people mentioned: Mary Saunders, deceased daughter; Susannah Winter Hanmer, deceased daughter; Elizabeth Winter Preston, deceased daughter; John Saunders, husband of Mary; Louisa Saunders Budden, grand-daughter; Heber Budden, husband of Louisa; Caroline Saunders, grand-daughter; Isabella Saunders, grand-daughter; Jessie Saunders Budden, grand-daughter; William Budden, husband of Jessie; Maria Saunders, grand-daughter; William Strachan, deceased son of Mary; H.W. Hanmer, grandchild of deceased, child of Susannah; L. Hanmer, grandchild of deceased, child of Susannah; C. Preston, grandchild of deceased, child of Elizabeth.

Summary: Meaning of the words "issue" and "lawful issue".

Location: Decisions of the Supreme Court of NL, 1884-1896, page 26

84 Name of case: In the Matter of the Will of the late Robert Alexander, Merchant

Date of case: April, 1885

Name of deceased: Robert Alexander

Date of death: Not given in the report

Other people mentioned: None

Summary: Testator left a gift to a society that didn't exist. The court admitted extrinsic evidence to discover the testator's intentions.

Location: Decisions of the Supreme Court of NL, 1884-1896, page 42

85 Name of case: Duder vs. Duder

Date of case: March, 1884

Name of deceased: Mary Elizabeth Duder

Date of death: December, 1881

Other people mentioned: Edwin John Duder, son, executor; Arthur George Duder, son, executor; Isabel Duder, widow of Arthur George.

Summary: Court said that a beneficiary who was conceived but not yet born at the time of the testator's death was considered alive at the time of the testator's death.

Location: Decisions of the Supreme Court of NL, 1884-1896, page 10

86 Name of case: Mosedale, et al. vs. McDougall, et al.

Date of case: March, 1893

Name of deceased: Henry Ledrew

Date of death: January, 1882

Other people mentioned: Ellen Skeans, daughter; William Skeans, husband of Ellen; Mary Ann Ledrew, wife; Isabella Mosedale, daughter; William Mosedale, husband of Isabella.

Summary: Disagreement over where the estate of a deceased beneficiary should go.

Location: Decisions of the Supreme Court of NL, 1884-1896, page 732

87 Name of case: K.R. Prowse, et al. vs. A.W. Harvey, et al

Date of case: September, 1896

Name of deceased: Edwin J. Duder

Date of death: 1881

Other people mentioned: Edwin John Duder, son; John Duder, son; Arthur George Duder, son; Harriet Elizabeth Duder, daughter; Isabella Duder, administratrix of the estate.

Summary: Court determination of where estate should go when all of named beneficiaries had passed away.

Location: Decisions of the Supreme Court of NL, 1884-1896, page 869

88   Name of case: In re Will of John Ashley

Date of case: 1890

Name of deceased: John Ashley

Date of death: Not given in the report

Other people mentioned: Daniel Ashley, son, executor; John Angel, executor; Mr. Morison, solicitor, witness to will; Ellen Ashley, daughter; J.C. Carter, accountant, witness to will; Rev. Mr. Crooke, witness; Rev. Mr. Ryan, witness; William Ashley, son; Mr. Pittman, solicitor, witness, Mr. Berteau, law student, witness.

Summary: In deciding testamentary capacity, it is the soundness of the testator's mind that counts, not the condition of his body.

Location: Decisions of the Supreme Court of NL, 1884-1896, page 447

89   Name of case: In re Estate Edwin Duder

Date of case: April, 1887

Name of deceased: Edwin Duder

Date of death: February, 1881

Other people mentioned: Edwin John Duder, son; Arthur George Duder, son; Harriet Elizabeth Ann Duder, daughter.

Summary: Question regarding the interpretation of terms of a will.

Location: Decisions of the Supreme Court of NL, 1884-1896, page 186

90   Name of case: Pike vs. Renouf

Date of case: April 5, 1900

Name of deceased: John Renouf

Date of death: Not given in the report

Other people mentioned: Ms. Pike, beneficiary;

Summary: In an action against an executor for an accounting where the executor does not appear in court, the plaintiff can get an order for the accounting.

Location: Decisions of the Supreme Court of NL, 1897-1903, page 369

91 Name of case: Purchase vs. Pitman

Date of case: June 12, 1901

Name of deceased: Robert Purchase

Date of death: January 7, 1895

Other people mentioned: None

Summary: Executor who delayed paying a bequest had to personally pay interest.

Location: Decisions of the Supreme Court of NL, 1897-1903, page 469

92 Name of case: In Re Southcott's Estate

Date of case: December 15, 1903

Name of deceased: James T. Southcott

Date of death: April 19, 1898

Other people mentioned: George T. Rendell, executor; Arthur S. Rendell, executor.

Summary: Executor's aren't automatically entitled to remuneration but the court may award it in cases of greater than usual difficulty.

Location: Decisions of the Supreme Court of NL, 1897-1903, page 645

93 Name of case: Adams vs. Knowling

Date of case: January 13, 1900

Name of deceased: Rev. Henry Petley

Date of death: January 23, 1898

Other people mentioned: Honourable George Knowling, trustee; Rev. Arthur H. Brown, trustee; George J. Adams, registrar, administrator of estate.

Summary: Property under a will had already been given to different trustees and a different arrangement.

Location: Decisions of the Supreme Court of NL, 1897-1903, page 351

94 Name of case: Bastow, Administrator vs. Radford, Administrator

Date of case: January, 1898

Name of deceased: Thomas Radford

Date of death: 1883

Other people mentioned: Lydia Bastow, daughter; Francis Bastow, administrator of Lydia's estate; Henry Thomas Bastow, son.

Summary: A bequest in a will is void if it is too vague.

Location: Decisions of the Supreme Court of NL, 1897-1903, page 66

95 Name of case: Monroe vs. McNeil, Executor

Date of case: January, 1898 and March 15, 1902

Name of deceased: Moses Monroe

Date of death: Not given in the report

Other people mentioned: Robert K. Bishop, business partner; Jessie Gordon Monroe; John Monroe; John McNeil, executor; Alfred G. Smith, trustee; James S. Pitts, trustee; Walter S. Monroe, executor.

Summary: Disposal in a will of assets that belonged to a business partnership.

Location: Decisions of the Supreme Court of NL, 1897-1903, page 95 and 545

96 Name of case: Roman Catholic Episcopal Corporation of St. John's vs. Pinsent

Date of case: June 11, 1900

Name of deceased: Catherine Wrey

Date of death: 1873

Other people mentioned: Bridget Frances Hunter, daughter; Rev. John Ryan, beneficiary; Priscilla Newman, friend, beneficiary; James Newman, husband of Priscilla; Right Rev. Thomas Joseph Power, beneficiary; Richard Wrey, husband;

Summary: Question whether a bequest with conditions vested in the beneficiary.

Location: Decisions of the Supreme Court of NL, 1897-1903, page 371

97 Name of case: In Re Angel's Trust

Date of case: October 1, 1907

Name of deceased: John Angel

Date of death: November, 1906

Other people mentioned: Elizabeth Ann Angel, first wife; William Angel, son of first marriage; Jenny Angel, daughter of first marriage; Annie Angel, daughter of first marriage; Lionel T. Chancey, trustee; Jane Angel, second wife; Mabel Angel, daughter of second marriage; Ethel Angel, daughter of second marriage; Marion Angel, daughter of second marriage; Gladys Angel, daughter of second marriage;

Summary: Question of whether a trust for wife and children extends to second wife of testator.

Location: Decisions of the Supreme Court of NL, 1904-1911, page 353

98 Name of case: Horwood vs. Milligan

Date of case: January 13, 1910

Name of deceased: Rev. George S. Milligan

Date of death: January 23, 1902

Other people mentioned: Julia S. Abraham, daughter; Archibald H. Milligan, son;

George S. Milligan, son.

Summary: A father's expense to set up his son in business was considered to be an advance on the son's inheritance.

Location: Decisions of the Supreme Court of NL, 1904-1911, page 439

99 Name of case: Jerrett vs. Jerrett

Date of case: June 8, 1905 and February 9, 1906

Name of deceased: George C. Jerrett

Date of death: 1904

Other people mentioned: Frederick Jerrett, son; Charles Jerrett, son.

Summary: Question whether a trust was validly created.

Location: Decisions of the Supreme Court of NL, 1904-1911, page 156

100 Name of case: In Re William Ford Tapp, Deceased, Ward vs. Tapp

Date of case: March 22, 1904

Name of deceased: William Ford Tapp

Date of death: Not given in the record

Other people mentioned: Hannah Tapp, widow; John Tapp, son; Nellie Tapp, daughter; Stanley Tapp, son; Melina Blackwood; daughter; George Tapp, son; Elfrida Tapp, daughter; Mary Jane Tapp, daughter; Anne Tapp.

Summary: Court construction of an unclear gift to the widow under a will.

Location: Decisions of the Supreme Court of NL, 1904-1911, page 18

101 Name of case: Murphy vs. Murphy

Date of case: January 24, 1905

Name of deceased: Martin Murphy

Date of death: February 28, 1904

Other people mentioned: Charles Murphy, executor; John Jenkinson, father-in-law of Charles; Richard Murphy.

Summary: A defendant who does not intend to call witnesses in proof of will should give notice to plaintiff.

Location: Decisions of the Supreme Court of NL, 1904-1911, page 78

102 Name of case: In Re James Furlong, Deceased, Howley vs. Furlong

Date of case: April 13, 1905

Name of deceased: James Furlong

Date of death: April, 1856

Other people mentioned: Margaret Furlong, widow; Elizabeth Dearin, daughter; Mary Furlong, daughter; Susan Furlong, daughter; James P. Furlong, son; Catherine S. Keough, daughter; John T. Furlong, son; Johanna Furlong, daughter; L. O'B. Furlong, son; Albert F. Dearin, grandson.

Summary: Question as to owned an annuity once the beneficiary passed away.

Location: Decisions of the Supreme Court of NL, 1904-1911, page 154

103 Name of case: In Re James Blundon, Deceased, Blundon vs. Blundon

Date of case: February 10, 1906

Name of deceased: James Blundon

Date of death: Approximately 1843

Other people mentioned: James Blundon, son; Tamar Blundon, daughter; John Blundon, son; John Blundon, grandson; Henry Blundon, grandson; James Blundon, grandson.

Summary: Question as to discretion of executor based on wording of will.

Location: Decisions of the Supreme Court of NL, 1904-1911, page 178

104 Name of case: Mullowney v. King

Date of case: February 12, 1906

Name of deceased: Francis Mullowney

Date of death: December 11, 1904

Other people mentioned: Catherine Mullowney, daughter, executor; Isabel Georgina MacPherson, adopted daughter, executor; Mary King, daughter.

Summary: A plaintiff who pleads fraud and undue influence during proof in solemn form then withdraws them at the last moment must pay costs.

Location: Decisions of the Supreme Court of NL, 1904-1911, page 182

105 Name of case: In re Martin Walsh, Kent vs. Power

Date of case: October 4, 1906

Name of deceased: Martin Walsh

Date of death: February 28, 1885

Other people mentioned: Robert Cole, nephew; Ellen Cole, sister; Bridget Cole, niece, daughter of Ellen; Kate Power, daughter of Ellen; Mary Wyse, sister; Bridget Whelan, sister; Annie Donovan, daughter of Mary; Catherine Power, daughter of Mary.

Summary: Question whether annuities under will were perpetual.

Location: Decisions of the Supreme Court of NL, 1904-1911, page 205

106 Name of case: Hugh Baird et al Executors vs. Attorney General

Date of case: 1915

Name of deceased: Honourable James Baird

Date of death: May 30, 1915

Other people mentioned: Hugh Baird.

Summary: Question whether old or new Death Duties Act applied.

Location: Decisions of the Supreme Court of NL, 1912-1920, page 159

107 Name of case: T.R. Job's Executors vs. Attorney General

Date of case: April, 1918

Name of deceased: Thomas R. Job

Date of death: May 19, 1917

Other people mentioned: None

Summary: Question whether death duties applied to land in NL owned by a deceased in England.

Location: Decisions of the Supreme Court of NL, 1912-1920, page 310

108 Name of case: Murphy vs. Star of the Sea Association

Date of case: January 1918

Name of deceased: Thomas Murphy

Date of death: Not given in the report

Other people mentioned: Katherine Murphy, widow.

Summary: Question whether the widow of a member should receive the original amount of life insurance subscribed for or a lesser amount.

Location: Decisions of the Supreme Court of NL, 1912-1920, page 268

109 Name of case: McCarthy vs. Brien et al

Date of case: May 1916

Name of deceased: Joseph Brien

Date of death: February, 1916

Other people mentioned: Dr. Mitchell, attending physician; Patrick Cahill, friend; Walter Power, witness; Michael Doran, witness; James Brien, brother; William Wyllie, witness.

Summary: When a will has been impeached on the ground of unsound mind, the onus is on the person setting up the will to prove its validity.

Location: Decisions of the Supreme Court of NL, 1912-1920, page 175

110 Name of case: Re Hennebury, Emerson, Administrator vs. Butler, Administrator

Date of case: 1917

Name of deceased: Richard Hennebury

Date of death: Approximately 1877

Other people mentioned: Mark Hennebury, son; James Hennebury, son; Patrick Hennebury, son; Richard Hennebury, son; James Daley, book-keeper; Bridget Daley, God-child.

Summary: Question of interpretation of an unclear clause in a will.

Location: Decisions of the Supreme Court of NL, 1912-1920, page 233

111 Name of case: In re will of Norman Outerbridge, Deceased

Date of case: October, 1918

Name of deceased: Norman Outerbridge

Date of death: Not given in the report

Other people mentioned: None

Summary: A corporation may not be appointed as an executor.

Location: Decisions of the Supreme Court of NL, 1912-1920, page 327

112 Name of case: In re Estate of David Hickey

Date of case: August 14, 1920

Name of deceased: David Hickey

Date of death: November, 1918

Other people mentioned: Elizabeth Walsh (formerly Elizabeth Hickey), widow, administrator.

Summary: Question whether a trust for first wife and children extended to second wife and children.

Location: Decisions of the Supreme Court of NL, 1912-1920, page 489

113 Name of case: Philip Templeman Ltd. vs. Bradshaw

Date of case: October, 1928

Name of deceased: Honourable Philip Templeman

Date of death: Not given in the record

Other people mentioned: None

Summary: Question whether a business owned by the deceased formed part of his estate.

Location: Decisions of the Supreme Court of NL, 1927-1931, page 183

114 Name of case: In re Carter; Royal Trust Company et al vs. Henderson et al

Date of case: January, 1927

Name of deceased: James Carter

Date of death: May 10, 1925

Other people mentioned: Lucretia Carter.

Summary: Death duties in NL and abroad should be paid from residue of estate and not from specific gifts.

Location: Decisions of the Supreme Court of NL, 1927-1931, page 3

115 Name of case: Finlay vs. Bishop et al

Date of case: July, 1931

Name of deceased: Robert K. Bishop

Date of death: Not given in the record

Other people mentioned: Bertha A. Finlay, sister-in-law.

Summary: A deed referenced under an old will was still valid because it was put into place before the new will was made.

Location: Decisions of the Supreme Court of NL, 1927-1931, page 514

116 Name of case: McGrath vs. Furlong

Date of case: October, 1929

Name of deceased: James J. McGrath

Date of death: April 19, 1927

Other people mentioned: Thomas F. McGrath, brother; Francis T. McGrath, son of Thomas; William J. McGrath, son of Thomas; Thomas M. McGrath, son of Thomas; Mary McGrath, daughter of Thomas; Caroline Furlong, beneficiary; Marion Furlong, beneficiary; Joyce Furlong, beneficiary; Robert Stafford Furlong, beneficiary; James E. McGrath, beneficiary; Thomas Scanlon McGrath, beneficiary; Michael Manning, court-appointed guardian for Thomas M. McGrath and Mary McGrath; Minnie Furlong, court-appointed guardian for Joyce Furlong.

Summary: Question as to who had to pay expenses for upkeep of a property with a life estate.

Location: Decisions of the Supreme Court of NL, 1927-1931, page 348

117 Name of case: Royal Trust Co. vs. Browning et al

Date of case: September, 1931

Name of deceased: Mary Browning and Elizabeth Browning

Date of death: Mary, May 8, 1929 ; Elizabeth August 24, 1929

Other people mentioned: James H. Browning; Gilbert Browning; James Crawford.

Summary: The amount of fees set down by the Trustee Act does not mean that all executors must be paid according to a percentage.

Location: Decisions of the Supreme Court of NL, 1927-1931, page 535

118 Name of case: In re Bond; Bond vs. Bond et al

Date: January, 1928

Name of deceased: Sir Robert Bond

Date of death: March 16, 1927

Other people mentioned: F. Fraser Bond, nephew; Roberta Bond Nichols, niece;

Reverend George John Bond, brother, executor.

Summary: In Newfoundland, lands are chattels and therefore an entail cannot apply.

Location: Decisions of the Supreme Court of NL, 1927-1931, page 109

119 Name of case: In re Heale; Lloyd vs. Bendell et al

Date of case: January, 1928

Name of deceased: Mary Ann Heale and Emma Heale

Date of death: Mary Ann, July 17, 1904; Emma March 16, 1927

Other people mentioned: Emma Heale, daughter of Mary Ann; Frances Bendell.

Summary: Question of interpretation of an unclear clause in a will.

Location: Decisions of the Supreme Court of NL, 1927-1931, page 131

120 Name of case: In re Ashley; McDermott vs. Fitzpatrick et al

Date of case: June, 1928

Name of deceased: John T. Ashley

Date of death: Not given in the record

Other people mentioned: Miss Fitzpatrick, housekeeper.

Summary: Question of interpretation of an unclear clause in a will regarding a gift to a housekeeper.

Location: Decisions of the Supreme Court of NL, 1927-1931, page 168

121 Name of case: In re Nowlan; Neville vs. Neville

Date of case: October, 1928

Name of deceased: Denis Nowlan and Peter Neville

Date of death: Denis, February 13, 1876; Peter October 22, 1925

Other people mentioned: Catherine Nowlan, wife of Denis; Peter Neville, son-in-law to Denis, executor for Denis; Mary Neville, first wife of Peter, daughter of Denis; John J. Neville, son of Peter, administrator for Peter; Denis Neville, son of Peter; Patrick J. Neville, son of Peter; Joseph Neville, son of Peter; Catherine Walsh, second wife of Peter; Emily M. Murphy, daughter of Peter.

Summary: Determination of the shares of children of man who married twice.

Location: Decisions of the Supreme Court of NL, 1927-1931, page 174

122 Name of case: In re Baird; London City & Midland Bank vs. Baird et al

Date of case: December, 1928

Name of deceased: Hugh Baird and John Maxwell Poole Baird

Date of death: Hugh, February 20, 1922; John, June 26, 1927

Other people mentioned: Madeline Baird, wife; John Maxwell Poole Baird, son of Hugh; James C. Baird, brother of Hugh; Annie Jessie Carter, sister of Hugh; David Baird, brother of Hugh; Margaret Baird, wife of John M.P. Baird; Cyril B. Carter, son of Annie.

Summary: Question of interpretation of an unclear clause in a will.

Location: Decisions of the Supreme Court of NL, 1927-1931, page 231

123 Name of case: Hickey vs. Hickey

Date of case: November, 1929

Name of deceased: Patrick Hickey

Date of death: August 15, 1928

Other people mentioned: Maria Hickey, wife; James Hickey, son; Michael Hickey, son; David Hickey, son; Thomas Hickey, son.

Summary: Son claimed that land in estate had been purchased from father before father died.

Location: Decisions of the Supreme Court of NL, 1927-1931, page 351

124 Name of case: In re Dawe; Dawe vs. Smith

Date of case: March, 1930

Name of deceased: Azariah Dawe

Date of death: January 8, 1919

Other people mentioned: William Fraser Dawe, son.

Summary: Question of interpretation of an unclear clause in a will.

Location: Decisions of the Supreme Court of NL, 1927-1931, page 388

125 In re Davey; Fletcher vs. Waugh et al

Date of case: May 1930

Name of deceased: George A. Davey

Date of death: May 7, 1920

Other people mentioned: James Augustus Clift, executor; James Waugh; Edward Waugh; Mary Waugh; Sarah Waugh.

Summary: Question of identifying a beneficiary whose name was correct but his parentage was incorrectly described in the will.

Location: Decisions of the Supreme Court of NL, 1927-1931, page 414

126 Name of case: In re McGrath; McGrath vs. McGrath

Date of case: June, 1930

Name of deceased: James J. McGrath

Date of death: April 19, 1927

Other people mentioned: Thomas Scanlon McGrath; Thomas F. McGrath, brother; Francis T. McGrath, son of Thomas F. McGrath.

Summary: Question re life tenancy with power of appointment.

Location: Decisions of the Supreme Court of NL, 1927-1931, page 444

127 Name of case: Courage vs. Courage

Date of case: December, 1931

Name of deceased: John Courage Sr.

Date of death: February 21, 1894

Other people mentioned: George Courage, nephew, executor for John Sr.; Reuben Courage, son; John Courage Jr, son; Elizabeth Soper, daughter; Ann Courage, wife of John Jr; Rachel Norman, daughter; Isaac J. Mifflin, witness; William J. Pomeroy, witness; Frederick C. Snelgrove, witness; Thomas Soper, son-in-law.

Summary: A will may be proved by one witness if that witness' veracity and competence are unimpeached.

Location: Decisions of the Supreme Court of NL, 1927-1931, page 549

128 Name of case: Harris vs. Newfoundland Railway

Date of case: February, 1928

Name of deceased: Harold Harris

Date of death: July 1, 1927

Other people mentioned: None

Summary: Question whether there was a dependency on the deceased for Workmen's Compensation.

Location: Decisions of the Supreme Court of NL, 1927-1931, page 146

129 Name of case: In re Harry J. Crowe, Deceased

Date of case: June, 1933

Name of deceased: Harry Judson Crowe

Date of death: May 25, 1928

Other people mentioned: None

Summary: The executor appealed the value of the estate put on by the Minister for purposes of determining death duties.

Location: Decisions of the Supreme Court of NL, 1932-1935, page 105

130 Name of case: In re Jean F.G. Penny, a Minor

Date of case: December, 1935

Name of deceased: Laura Greening

Date of death: June 26, 1934

Other people mentioned: Jean F. Greening Penny, niece of Laura; Albert G. Penny, father of Jean; Jeddy G. Penny, mother of Jean; John T. Butler, friend of Laura; Janet Butler, wife of John, friend of Laura.

Summary: A child was to receive a legacy if raised by certain relatives. Parents took child back. Relatives sued for custody of the child.

Location: Decisions of the Supreme Court of NL, 1932-1935, page 383 and 393

131 Name of case: Sullivan vs. Baldwin

Date of case: February, 1935

Name of deceased: Edward Sullivan

Date of death: Jul.y16, 1934

Other people mentioned: Joseph Baldwin, executor; David Sullivan, grandson; Rev. J.A. Meaden, witness; Ernest Sullivan, son.

Summary: Grandfather added grandson to his bank account. Question of who owned the account on the death of the grandfather.

Location: Decisions of the Supreme Court of NL, 1932-1935, page 291

132 Name of case: In re Will of W.A. Bradbury, Deceased: Bradbury et al vs. Bradbury

Date of case: February, 1935

Name of deceased: William A. Bradbury

Date of death: October 11, 1932

Other people mentioned: Mary Rebecca Bradbury, widow; Samuel Bradbury, executor; Mary Wilmot Dawe, daughter; John D. Dawe, husband of Mary Wilmot; Malcolm Stanley Bradbury, grandson; Elizabeth Jane Vacheresse, daughter of Mary Rebecca.

Summary: Husband added wife to his bank account for convenience. Question of who owned the account on the death of the husband.

Location: Decisions of the Supreme Court of NL, 1932-1935, page 284

133 Name of case: Butler, Administrator of Reddy vs. Reddy

Date of case: November, 1934

Name of deceased: Michael Reddy

Date of death: June, 1911

Other people mentioned: Thomas Reddy, son; Michael Reddy, son.

Summary: Power of appointment failed because it was made in a will that was faulty.

Location: Decisions of the Supreme Court of NL, 1932-1935, page 217

134 Name of case: In re Neal's Estate

Date of case: October, 1933

Name of deceased: Not given in the record

Date of death: Not given in the record

Other people mentioned: Elsie Neal, beneficiary; Phyllis Neal, beneficiary; Edith Neal; beneficiary.

Summary: Determination of the appropriate amount of executor compensation.

Location: Decisions of the Supreme Court of NL, 1932-1935, page 108

135 Name of case: In re Coleman

Date of case: January, 1934

Name of deceased: John Coleman Sr.

Date of death: 1852

Other people mentioned: Robert J. Coleman, grandson (son of John Jr); Catherine Coleman, widow; John Coleman Jr, son; Julia Coleman, daughter; Charles

H. Hutchings, administrator of the estate of George Winter; John Murch Brine, administrator of the estate of George Winter.

Summary: Quieting of titles respecting land held in an estate.

Location: Decisions of the Supreme Court of NL, 1932-1935, page 139. Appeal page 149.

136 Name of case: Somerton vs. Somerton

Date of case: April, 1935

Name of deceased: Matthew Somerton

Date of death: Not given in the record

Other people mentioned: Maria Somerton, wife.

Summary: Interpretation of unclear wording in a will.

Location: Decisions of the Supreme Court of NL, 1932-1935, page 315

137 Name of case: In re Jackson; Meaden vs. Lloyd, Administrators

Date of case: March, 1935

Name of deceased: Edward Doyle Jackson

Date of death: February 10, 1913

Other people mentioned: Alexander Jackson, father; Delphine Jackson, mother.

Summary: Question whether the executors had proved testator had capacity to make a will.

Location: Decisions of the Supreme Court of NL, 1932-1935, page 299

138 Name of case: In re Mitchell; McGrath vs. Henley

Date of case: January, 1932

Name of deceased: Elizabeth Mitchell

Date of death: May 21, 1888

Other people mentioned: Timothy Mitchell, husband; Peter Mitchell, son; Michael Mitchell, son; Thomas Mitchell, administrator of estate; Theresa Mitchell; John J. Henley.

Summary: Interpretation of an unclear clause in a will.

Location: Decisions of the Supreme Court of NL, 1932-1935, page 9

139   Name of case: In re Woods; Woods vs. Woods et al.

Date of case: October, 1933

Name of deceased: John Woods

Date of death: May 2, 1896

Other people mentioned: Henry J.B. Woods, son; Frederick Woods, son; Alfred Woods, son; Edwin Woods, son; Sidney Woods, son; Chesley Woods, son; Emily Bulley, daughter; Anna Pippy, daughter; William Crescombe Woods, son; Florence Woods, daughter of William; James Brine, leaseholder; Elizabeth Hunt, administrator of the estate of James Brine; William Newman, leaseholder; Robert S. Pinsent, administrator of the estate of Williamm Newman; Henry Adams, leaseholder; George T. Rendell, administrator of the estate of Henry Adams.

Summary: Question whether alienation clauses in a will were enforceable.

Location: Decisions of the Supreme Court of NL, 1932-1935, page 109

140   Name of case: In re Mary Walsh, Deceased; Parker, Executor vs. Renouf

Date of case:

Name of deceased: Mary Walsh

Date of death: December 31, 1927

Other people mentioned: Robert Walsh, husband; John S. Keating, executor; John J. Parker.

Summary: An executor had discretion to make charitable gifts from a will but stepped down before doing so. New executor was appointed by the court and powers determined.

Location: Decisions of the Supreme Court of NL, 1932-1935, page 281

141 Name of case: In re Russell; Carivan vs. Russell

Date of case: Nov. 1933

Name of deceased: John Russell

Date of death: May 15, 1929

Other people mentioned: Emma Russell, daughter; Eva Russell, daughter; George Russell, brother; Nathan Russell, son of George;

Summary: Interpretation of an unclear clause in a will.

Location: Decisions of the Supreme Court of NL, 1932-1935, page 136

142 Name of case: Kavanagh vs. Eastern Trust Co. et al

Date of case: May, 1932

Name of deceased: Thomas F. Kavanagh

Date of death: November 2, 1931

Other people mentioned: Reverend John Kavanagh, son; Elizabeth Kavanagh, widow; Madeline Sutton, witness; Minnie Doutney, witness; Garrett Kavanagh, brother.

Summary: Determination of whether testator had requisite testamentary capacity.

Location: Decisions of the Supreme Court of NL, 1932-1935, page 22

143 Name of case: Whitty et al vs. Butler, Administrator for Whitty

Date of case: January, 1940

Name of deceased: James Whitty Sr

Date of death: February, 1938

Other people mentioned: James Whitty Jr, son; Frances, wife of James Jr; John Thomas Whitty, son; Patrick Whitty, son; Francis Whitty, son; Mary Tapper, daughter.

Summary: An uncorroborated claim against the estate of a deceased person could not stand.

144 Name of case: Hackett vs. Burling, Administrator of Lyons

Date of case: April, 1939

Name of deceased: Mr. Lyons

Date of death: 1938

Other people mentioned: None

Summary: An uncorroborated claim against the estate of a deceased person could not stand.

Location: Decisions of the Supreme Court of NL, 1936-1940, page 252

145 Name of case: Cashin vs. Cashin

Date of case: June, 1936 and January, 1937

Name of deceased: Sir Michael P. Cashin

Date of death: August 30, 1926

Other people mentioned: Lawrence V. Cashin, son, executor; Peter J. Cashin, son; Gertrude C. Cashin, widow, executrix; Martin Cashin, son; Mr. C.J. Fox, son-in-law.

Summary: Clarification of the fiduciary relationship between and executor and beneficiary.

Location: Decisions of the Supreme Court of NL, 1936-1940, page 42 and 72

146 Name of case: In re Milley; Butt vs. Butt et al

Date of case: November, 1938

Name of deceased: Alexander Milley

Date of death: Not given in the record

Other people mentioned: Bertha Cook, niece; William Milley, nephew; Jesse Butt, plaintiff, executor; Myrtle King, servant, witness, John Crummey, farmer, witness; Olive Cooper, servant, witness.

Summary: Determination of whether there was undue influence by the residuary beneficiaries.

Location: Decisions of the Supreme Court of NL, 1936-1940, page 181

147 Name of case: Crotty vs. Crotty

Date of case: December, 1938

Name of deceased: Maurice Crotty, Sr.

Date of death: February, 1893

Other people mentioned: Mary Crotty, daughter; John Crotty, son; Margaret Crotty, daughter; Ellen Crotty, daughter; Bridget Crotty, daughter; Patrick Crotty, son; Thomas Crotty, son; William Crotty, son; Maurice Crotty, Jr, son.

Summary: Executor held onto estate land for 20 years.

Location: Decisions of the Supreme Court of NL, 1936-1940, page 208

148 Name of case: Manuel vs. Rice

Date of case: December, 1938

Name of deceased: Amelia Rice

Date of death: 1917

Other people mentioned: Joseph Rice, husband; David Rice, son; George Rice, son; Arthur Rice, son.

Summary: Determination of what husband owned on death of wife when Married Women's Property Act came into force around the same time.

Location: Decisions of the Supreme Court of NL, 1936-1940, page 204

149 Name of case: Butler vs. Dominion Steel and Coal Ltd

Date of case: December, 1939

Name of deceased: Thomas Butler

Date of death: June 22, 1939

Other people mentioned: Mr. Archibald, manager at the company; Mr. Proudfoot, assistant manager; Mr. Gilliatt, chief engineer.

Summary: Whether there was negligence by the employer of a 17-year-old boy killed on the job.

Location: Decisions of the Supreme Court of NL, 1936-1940, page 296

150 Name of case: In re Alderdice and Johnstone

Date of case: March, 1940

Name of deceased: Not given in the record

Date of death: Not given in the record

Other people mentioned: None

Summary: Question regarding how trust companies should account for legacies from different sources, and whether can pay themselves remuneration without court order.

Location: Decisions of the Supreme Court of NL, 1936-1940, page 337

151 Name of case: Midstream Realty Co. vs. Deane

Date of case: December, 1936

Name of deceased: Thomas H. Walters Sr.

Date of death: Not given in the record

Other people mentioned: Mary Grace Smith, daughter; James Thomas Smith, husband of Mary Grace; Cyril J. Smith, grandson; Thomas H. Walters Jr, son, Trustee; Charles Bowring, trustee.

Summary: Interpretation of bequest when the testator had several more children after making his will.

Location: Decisions of the Supreme Court of NL, 1936-1940, page 60

152 Name of case: John G. Munn, Deceased: Munn vs Munn

Date of case: June, 1936

Name of deceased: John G. Munn Jr.

Date of death: 1935

Other people mentioned: Mary Edina Munn, first wife; Elizabeth Munn, mother; George T. Brown, grandfather; John Munn Sr, father; Norman Munn, son; Jean Munn Baggs, daughter; Frank Munn, son; Christina Munn, second wife of deceased.

Summary: Interpretation of an unclear clause in a will.

Location: Decisions of the Supreme Court of NL, 1936-1940, page 35

153 Name of case: Stahler et al vs. Harvey

Date of case: September, 1937

Name of deceased: Alexander John Harvey

Date of death: September 1, 1928

Other people mentioned: Reginald Cockburn Harvey, son; Gerald Cockburn Harvey; Harold Cockburn Harvey, son; Edith Cockburn Powys-Keck, daughter; Doris Wayne (also spelled Mayne) Stahler, daughter of Harold; Edith N. Harvey, daughter of Harold; Alexander Neilson Harvey, son of Harold.

Summary: Interpretation of an unclear clause in a will.

Location: Decisions of the Supreme Court of NL, 1936-1940, page 127

154 Name of case: Ball vs. Rowsell

Date of case: May 1937

Name of deceased: Albert Ball

Date of death: July 9, 1934

Other people mentioned: Julia Ball, widow; Elsie Rowsell, daughter; Harry Ball, son; Blanche Bannester, daughter of Harry.

Summary: Interpretation of an unclear clause in a will.

155 Name of case: Branscombe's Estates Ltd. vs. Barron, Executor for Carrigan

Date of case: December, 1940

Name of deceased: Peter Carrigan

Date of death: November 14, 1920

Other people mentioned: Elizabeth O'Neil, daughter; Mary Ann Collins, daughter; John A. Barron, executor.

Summary: Question regarding the effect of an executor agreeing to a life estate.

Location: Decisions of the Supreme Court of NL, 1936-1940, page 390

156 Name of case: Broderick vs. Mitchell

Date of case: November, 1937

Name of deceased: Theodore Broderick

Date of death: April 17, 1937

Other people mentioned: Annie Mitchell, daughter; John Broderick, brother; William H. Butt, witness; Jabez Butt, witness; E. Martin, witness; Winnifred Broderick, daughter.

Summary: Determination of whether the testator had testamentary capacity.

Location: Decisions of the Supreme Court of NL, 1936-1940, page 130

157 Name of case: In re Cave: Cave et al vs. Skinner

Date of case: December, 1938

Name of deceased: Captain Robert Dixon Cave

Date of death: June 22, 1922

Other people mentioned: Dora Susannah Cave, wife; J.A. Clift, trustee; Ernest Louis Cave; Gertrude Dora Cave Skinner, daughter; Florrie May Skinner, daughter; Captain F. Axford, witness; J.J. Murphy, witness; Evelyn Cave Hiscock.

Summary: Interpretation of how a will worked together with a deed of land where more land was acquired after making the deed.

Location: Decisions of the Supreme Court of NL, 1936-1940, page 212

158 Name of case: Flood vs. Flood

Date of case: December, 1940

Name of deceased: Edward Flood Sr

Date of death: November 27, 1927

Other people mentioned: Catherine Kirby, daughter; John Flood, son; Patrick Flood, son; William Flood, son; Edward Flood Jr, son; Gregory Flood, son; Joseph Flood, son; Matthew Flood, son; Thomas Flood, son; Leo Flood, son; Matthew O'Rourke, witness; Michael O'Rourke, witness; Thomas Hennessey, witness.

Summary: A will was lost but its contents were adequately proven.

Location: Decisions of the Supreme Court of NL, 1936-1940, page 397

159 Name of case: Flynn vs. Flynn

Date of case: November 6, 1937

Name of deceased: Patrick Flynn

Date of death: December 25, 1927

Other people mentioned: Alice Flynn, wife; Gregory Daniel Flynn, son; Mary Theresa Talbot, daughter; Bridget Philomena Flynn, daughter; Elizabeth Helena Flynn, daughter; Annie Christina Flynn, daughter; Patrick August Flynn, son; Cyril Flynn, witness; Daniel Flynn, witness.

Summary: Interpretation of unclear wording in a will.

Location: Decisions of the Supreme Court of NL, 1936-1940, page 136

160 Name of case: In re Fowler; Pike vs. Royal Bank of Canada and Howley, administrator

Date of case: January, 1938

Name of deceased: Esau Fowler

Date of death: 1913

Other people mentioned: John Fowler, brother; Charlotte Maud Fowler, step-daughter of John.

Summary: Interpretation of an unclear clause in a will.

Location: Decisions of the Supreme Court of NL, 1936-1940, page 158

161 Name of case: Carteret Lee vs. Patrick Williams

Date of case: January, 1940

Name of deceased: John Williams

Date of death: 1916

Other people mentioned: Matthew Williams, son; George Williams, son; Alan Williams, son; Daniel Clarke, landowner; Simon Clarke, landowner; Michael Hearn, landowner; Honourable Patrick Morris, landowner; Michael Flynn, landowner; John Kennedy, landowner; Richard Howlett, witness; Mrs. Stephen Donovan, witness, former wife of Michael Flynn; William Noel, former Minister of Agriculture; John Clarke, son of Simon, nephew of Daniel, witness.

Summary: Court determined that names in a will were phonetic spellings of certain people.

Location: Decisions of the Supreme Court of NL, 1936-1940, page 332

162 Name of case: In re Lowe; Lowe & Baggs vs. Lowe

Date of case: November, 1938

Name of deceased: George Lowe

Date of death: March 3, 1938

Other people mentioned: Sarah Lowe, widow; Arthur Lowe, son; Ernest Lowe, son; Frank Lowe, son; Cyril Lowe, son; Fred Lowe, son; Roy Lowe, son; Margaret

Meaney, daughter; Mildred Butt, daughter; Eva Lowe, daughter; Phyllis Lowe, daughter; Colleen Lowe, daughter; Joan Lowe, daughter; Walter Baggs, executor.

Summary: Interpretation of an unclear clause in a will.

Location: Decisions of the Supreme Court of NL, 1936-1940, page 195

163 Name of case: In re Percey; Percey vs. Percey

Date of case: August, 1939

Name of deceased: Nathan Percey Sr.

Date of death: 1883

Other people mentioned: Nathan Percey Jr, son; Stephen Percey Sr, son; Caroline Percey, daughter; Elizabeth Percey, daughter; Eliza Percey, daughter; Moses Payne, grandson; Stephen Percey Jr, grand son, son of Stephen Sr; Nathan Percey III, grandson; Mary Payne, daughter; Sarah Bartlett, daughter; Frances Pine, daughter; William Horwood, witness; James Whalen, witness; Mary Ann Percey, daughter of Nathan Jr.

Summary: Interpretation of an unclear clause in a will.

Location: Decisions of the Supreme Court of NL, 1936-1940, page 274

164 Name of case: Ryan et al vs. Ottenheimer et al

Date of case: May, 1937

Name of deceased: Daniel A. Ryan

Date of death: July 6, 1933

Other people mentioned: Margaret G. Ryan, widow; Edmund J. Ryan, brother;- John T. McCarthy, executor; Walter N. White, nephew; Margaret White, sister;- Frederick W. Ottenheimer, son-in-law.

Summary: Where a will and subsequent codicil are inconsistent with each other, the codicil revokes the applicable sections of the will.

Location: Decisions of the Supreme Court of NL, 1936-1940, page 111

165 Name of case: Ryan vs. Ryan

Date of case: May, 1937

Name of deceased: Nicholas Ryan

Date of death: Not given in the record

Other people mentioned: Anastatia Ryan; Irene MacDonald; James Sweeney; Ann Sweeney.

Summary: Where wills/documents are inconsistent, the second one prevails.

Location: Decisions of the Supreme Court of NL, 1936-1940, page 116

166 Name of case: In re Templeman; McCall vs. Saint and Oldford

Date of case: November, 1938

Name of deceased: Joseph Templeman

Date of death: May 8, 1930

Other people mentioned: Ann Templeman, mother; Deborah Templeman, sister; Priscilla Saint, sister; Sarah Oldford, sister; Irene McCall, sister.

Summary: Interpretation of an unclear clause in a will.

Location: Decisions of the Supreme Court of NL, 1936-1940, page 177

167 Name of case: Burden vs. Butler, Administrator of Bridle

Date of case: May 1941

Name of deceased: Laura S. Bridle

Date of death: Not given in the record

Other people mentioned: Rev. Burden, son-in-law.

Summary: Question whether a gift to a son-in-law was a true deathbed gift.

Location: Decisions of the Supreme Court of NL, 1941-1946, page 33

168 Name of case: In re Kennedy; Butler, Administrator for Dawe

Date of case: March, 1946

Name of deceased: John Kennedy

Date of death: Not given in the record

Other people mentioned: William Charles Kennedy, son; Samuel Kennedy, son; Esther Kennedy (later Esther Dawe), wife of William; Robert John Kennedy, grandchild, son of William; Selina Kennedy, daughter of William; Laura Kennedy, daughter of William.

Summary: Question of who owned land that had been held in trust.

Location: Decisions of the Supreme Court of NL, 1941-1946, page 424

169 Name of case: Nicholas J. Wadden vs. James Megann

Date of case: December, 1944

Name of deceased: W.B. Fitzgerald

Date of death: November 19, 1930

Other people mentioned: Nicholas J. Wadden, executor; Mary Fitzgerald, daughter; James Megann, tenant.

Summary: An executor continued to collect rent from tenant of deceased, creating a new tenancy.

Location: Decisions of the Supreme Court of NL, 1941-1946, page 291

170 Name of case: Aitken vs. Pollock and Pearcey

Date of case: April, 1945

Name of deceased: Alexander Aitken

Date of death: June, 1944

Other people mentioned: Ethel Aitken, widow; Pearl Aitken, daughter; Ruby Aitken, daughter.

Summary: Question of how to distribute funds between widow and children when negligence was the cause of death.

Location: Decisions of the Supreme Court of NL, 1941-1946, page 380

171 Name of case: In re Catherine Gaul, Deceased

Date of case: November, 1946

Name of deceased: Catherine Gaul

Date of death: March 21, 1907

Other people mentioned: Ellen Flynn, later Ellen Power, daughter; Edward O'Neil, grandson; Richard O'Neil, grandson; Sir Edward Morris, executor.

Summary: The estate sought compensation for expropriated land.

Location: Decisions of the Supreme Court of NL, 1941-1946, page 480

172 Name of case: In re Lynch: Alsop, Trustee vs. Garneau and Another

Date of case: December, 1945

Name of deceased: Mr. Lynch

Date of death: Not given in the record

Other people mentioned: Simon Butler, Deputy Registrar, trustee; Mr. Alsop, Registrar.

Summary: Question whether the appointment of the Registrar as trustee was ex officio or a personal appointment.

Location: Decisions of the Supreme Court of NL, 1941-1946, page 374

173 Name of case: In re McNeily

Date of case: November, 1943

Name of deceased: Not given in the record

Date of death: Not given in the record

Summary: Determination of remuneration for trustee.

Location: Decisions of the Supreme Court of NL, 1941-1946, page 171

174 Name of case: McGrath vs. The Royal Trust Company

Date of case: March, 1945

Name of deceased: T. Scanlon McGrath

Date of death: 1935

Other people mentioned: Alice McGrath, widow.

Summary: Request that the trust company in charge of estate funds should pay for the children's education in medicine and engineering.

Location: Decisions of the Supreme Court of NL, 1941-1946, page 381

175 Name of case: Montreal Trust Co vs. Power et al

Date of case: November, 1942

Name of deceased: Michael J. Power

Date of death: March 10, 1941

Other people mentioned: David Corbett Power, son; Mary Power, daughter; Robert Power, son.

Summary: Whether actions of the deceased while alive amounted to creation of an irrevocable trust.

Location: Decisions of the Supreme Court of NL, 1941-1946, page 109

176 Name of case: In re Wills of Elijah Burry and Mary Burry: Mifflin, Executor vs Cotton, Executor et al

Date of case: February, 1941

Name of deceased: Elijah Burry and Mary Burry

Date of death: Elijah, 1922; Mary, January 1, 1939

Other people mentioned: Eric Sparks, beneficiary; Nelson Sparks, father of Eric;- Frank D. Cotton, executor for Mary; I.J. Mifflin, executor for Elijah.

Summary: Question of which assets went to the widow as part of a life estate and which assets belonged to her outright.

Location: Decisions of the Supreme Court of NL, 1941-1946, page 3

177 Name of case: In re Aitken

Date of case: October 16, 1947

Name of deceased: Alexander Aitken

Date of death: June, 1944

Other people mentioned: Pearl Aitken, daughter; Ruby Aitken, daughter; Ethel Aitken, widow; William Stevenson, brother-in-law.

Summary: Question whether an estate trustee/widow could spend trust funds to buy a house for the children and herself to live in.

Location: Decisions of the Supreme Court of NL, 1947-1949, page 78

178 Name of case: Taylor et al vs. Nfld. Concrete Products Ltd. (McNamara Construction Co. Ltd. et al 3rd parties)

Date of case: January, 1947. Appeal from November, 1946

Name of decased: James Morgan Sr.

Date of death: 1911

Other people mentioned: James Morgan Jr., son; William Morgan, son; Emily Morgan, daughter; Ann Morgan, daughter; Gilbert Morgan, grandson, son of James Jr.

Summary: Father died intestate. Two sons worked the land to exclusion of sisters, thereby gaining adverse possession of it.

Location: Decisions of the Supreme Court of NL, 1947-1949, page 4

179 Name of case: Sullivan vs. Sullivan

Date of case: February, 1947

Name of deceased: Lawrence Sullivan

Date of death: 1915

Other people mentioned: Richard Sullivan, son, executor; Martin Sullivan, son, executor; Joseph Sullivan, son; John Sullivan, son; Kate Sullivan, daughter.

Summary: Question who can challenge the sale from one trustee to another.

Location: Decisions of the Supreme Court of NL, 1947-1949, page 16

180 Name of case: In re Harveys Trusts

Date of case: March, 1948

Name of deceased: Alexander John McRae Harvey

Date of death: September 1, 1928

Other people mentioned: Amy Constance Harvey, widow; Edith Mary Cockburn Powys-Keck, daughter; Clodagh Betty Lampson, grandchild, daughter of Edith; Gwladys J.M.J. Fenwick, grandchild, daughter of Edith; Gerald Cockburn Harvey, son; Harold Cockburn Harvey, son; Sally R.H. Voorhees, widow of Harold; Doris H. Stahler, grandchild, daughter of Harold; Edith Harvey Valentine, grandchild, daughter of Harold; Alexander Neilson Cockburn Harvey, grandchild, son of Harold; Reginald Cockburn Harvey, son.

Summary: Question of when to close a class of beneficiaries named in a will.

Location: Decisions of the Supreme Court of NL, 1947-1949, page 180 and 167

181 Name of case: Furlong vs. Hutchings

Date of case: August, 1947

Name of deceased: George Winter

Date of death: 1859

Other people mentioned: Charles H. Hutchings, administrator of estate; Frederick Winter, son, executor; Gordon W. Warren, lawyer, administrator of estate; Summary: An executor's job is to collect and distribute assets and not to make himself a manager of the property for 45 years.

Location: Decisions of the Supreme Court of NL, 1947-1949, page 73

182 Name of case: In re Bennett; Wyatt vs. Bennett et al

Date of case: April, 1947

Name of deceased: Louisa Ann Bennett

Date of death: July, 1926

Other people mentioned: Henry Wyatt, son-in-law, executor; Louisa Wyatt, daughter; Arthur Charles Bennett, son; Charles Fox Bennett, son; Elizabeth Mary Bennett, daughter; Minetta Fanny Pike, daughter; Edward Bennett, deceased husband.

Summary: Question as to which assets fall under description of "my personal property".

Location: Decisions of the Supreme Court of NL, 1947-1949, page 33

183 Name of case: In re Conroy: Deed

Date of case: January, 1947

Name of deceased: Charles O'Neill Conroy

Date of death: Not given in the record

Other people mentioned: Loius Conroy, son, executor; Harry Conroy, son, executor; Edward Conroy, son, executor.

Summary: Executors wanted to add an additional executor to carry on a trusteeship.

Location: Decisions of the Supreme Court of NL, 1947-1949, page 3

184 Name of case: Burke vs. Frampton

Date of case: May 1948

Name of deceased: Augusta Burke

Date of death: Not given in the record

Other people mentioned: Joseph Burke, husband; Edmund Frampton, brother-in-law; James Burke, adopted son;

Summary: Executor over-stepped his role by spending his own money to improve an estate property.

Location: Decisions of the Supreme Court of NL, 1947-1949, page 270

185 Name of case: Delaney vs. Corbett

Date of case: November, 1948

Name of deceased: Joseph Corbett

Date of death: June, 1948

Other people mentioned: Frank Corbett, son; Michael Corbett, nephew; Walter Delaney, friend, beneficiary; Bridget Delaney, wife of Walter.

Summary: Question whether a joint bank account led to a resulting trust.

Location: Decisions of the Supreme Court of NL, 1947-1949, page 341

186 Name of case: In re Bessie Dicks, Deceased

Date of case: February, 1948

Name of deceased: Bessie Dicks

Date of death: Not given in the record

Other people mentioned: George Peters, friend, executor; Maude Leamon, sister; John Leamon, brother-in-law; Maxwell Pratt, executor; Bertha Foot, sister; Eliza Radford, sister.

Summary: Question whether a second holograph will by a person of deteriorated capacity was a codicil or a replacement will.

Location: Decisions of the Supreme Court of NL, 1947-1949, page 160

187 Name of case: In re Ayre

Date of case: December, 1947

Name of deceased: F.W. Ayre

Date of death: 1932

Other people mentioned: Grace Ayre, widow; Sheila Ayre, daughter; Hartley Ayre, son.

Summary: Children of deceased applied for a distribution of estate even though their mother was still alive.

Location: Decisions of the Supreme Court of NL, 1947-1949, page 103

NOTES

www.ingramcontent.com/pod-product-compliance
Lightning Source LLC
Chambersburg PA
CBHW060337290526
45793CB00003B/647